This Little Explore The  book belongs to:

_____

For Curious Learners

© 2022 Grant Publishing

All rights reserved. No part of this publication may be reproduced, distributed or transmitted in any form or means without prior permission of the publisher.

Published by Grant Publishing

Sales and Enquires: grantpublishingltd@gmail.com

FOLLOW US ON SOCIAL MEDIA

 @grantpublishingltd

60 FACTS ABOUT GREECE

60 Facts About Greece

Hey, little explorers! Do you love learning about faraway places and cool facts? Well, have you heard about a land full of ancient gods, sparkling seas, and mouthwatering food? It's called Greece, and it's one of the most amazing countries in the world!

If you want to know more about Greece and its wonders, there's a super fun book you gotta check out. It's packed with cool facts that are easy to munch on, like yummy snacks, and it's got the most gorgeous photos you've ever seen! So grab a comfy seat and get ready to take a journey to Greece through the pages of this book!

For Parents

We know that reading a book about a new country can be an exciting adventure for your child. It's important to remember that kids need breaks, and may not want to read the book all in one sitting. Encourage them to take breaks as needed, and ask them questions about what they've learned so far. Discussing the facts with your child can help them remember and retain the information better. You can also use the book as a springboard for further exploration and learning about Greece. Perhaps you can plan a family outing to try some Greek food or visit a local museum with exhibits on ancient Greek culture. Above all, we hope that this book sparks your child's curiosity and inspires them to learn more about the world around them.

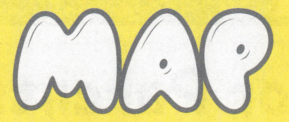

The Facts

1. Greece is a country in the continent of Europe!

2. Greece is situated in Southeast Europe.

EUROPE IS THE SECOND-SMALLEST CONTINENT IN TERMS OF LAND AREA, COVERING ONLY ABOUT 10.18 MILLION SQUARE KILOMETRES, WHICH IS ROUGHLY 2% OF THE EARTH'S SURFACE. DESPITE ITS SMALL SIZE, EUROPE IS THE THIRD-MOST POPULOUS CONTINENT

3. Greece shares borders with Albania, North Macedonia, Bulgaria and Turkey.

HOW MANY CAPTITAL CITIES CAN YOU THINK OF?

4. Athens is the capital city of Greece.

Pictured St Peter's Square, Athens

DID YOU KNOW?

Athens is the capital city of Greece and is one of the oldest cities in the world, with a history spanning over 3,400 years.

5. Athens is the largest city in Greece.

Pictured Parthenon Temple, Athens

6. Athens is named after the goddess Athena.

7. The second largest city in Greece is Thessaloniki

Pictured Thessaloniki City

8. The official language of Greece is Greek.

Sound out these phrases
Γεια σου (yia soo) - Hello
Ευχαριστώ (ef-kha-ri-sto) - Thank you
Τι κάνεις; (tee ka-nees) - How are you?

9. The national anthem of Greece is 'Ύμνος εις την Ελευθερίαν'.

10. Greek independence day is celebrated on 25th March.

11. Greece is a member state of the European Union.

> The European Union (EU) is a political and economic union of 27 member states located in Europe. The EU was established by the Treaty of Maastricht in 1993 with the goal of promoting peace, stability, and economic prosperity in Europe.

12. Greece has a population of over 10 million people.

13. Greece is the 85th most populous country in the world.

14. People from Greece are called Greek.

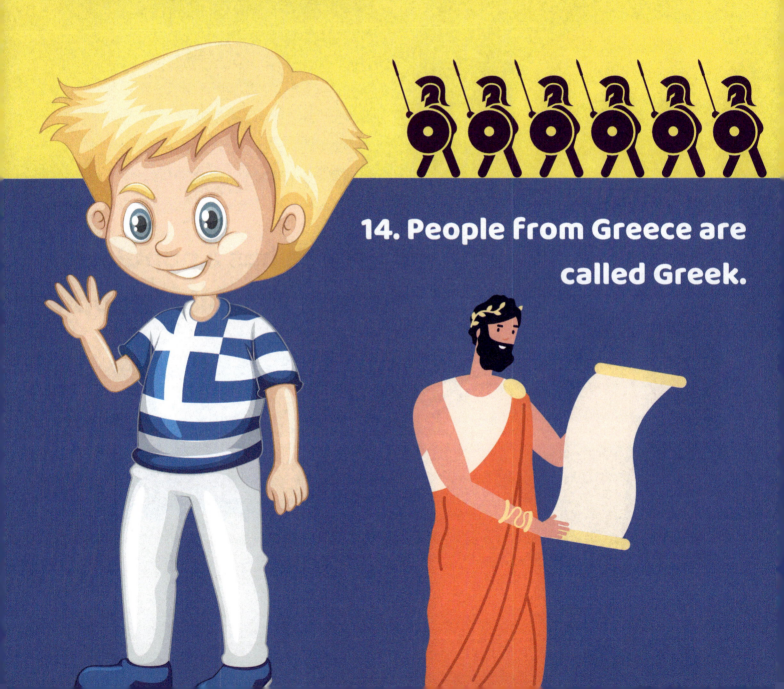

15. Greece is 131,957 square kilometres.

16. The currency is the Euro.

17. The national flag of Greece consists of nine horizontal stripes of blue and white with a blue canton bearing a white cross.

18. Greece is the birthplace of democracy, western philosophy, western literature, political science, theatre and the Olympic Games.

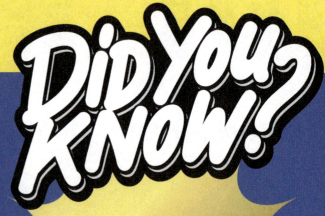

Did You Know?

The Olympic Games were first held in Olympia in 776 BCE and continued for over a thousand years until they were banned by the Roman Emperor Theodosius I in 393 CE.

19. Greece is also the birthplace of some major scientific and mathematic principles.

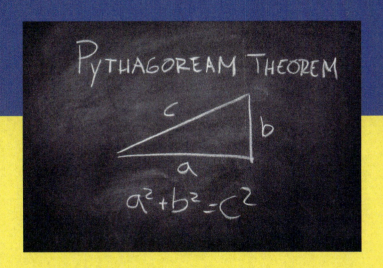

> The exact birthdate of Pythagoras is not known, but it is believed that he was born on the island of Samos, Greece, around 570 BCE. He lived until around 495 BCE

20. Greek mathematician, Pythagoras, was famous for his theorem and also came up with the value of pie.

21. Greece is famous for its beautiful beaches, such as Mykonos, Santorini, and Crete.

Pictured Santorini

22. Greek mythology has many famous gods and goddesses, such as Zeus, and Aphrodite.

> Zeus was known for his many romantic conquests and numerous affairs with mortal women and goddesses alike. He was said to have fathered many children, some of whom became famous heroes and demigods.

23. Greece is famous for its olives and olive oil.

Pictured olive Tree in Thassos Island

24. The highest mountain in Greece is Mount Olympus, which is also the mythical home of the gods.

Pictured Mount Olympus in Greece

25. Greece is known for its delicious food, such as moussaka, souvlaki, and gyros.

26. The Greek philosopher Aristotle was a student of Plato and a teacher of Alexander the Great.

Aristotle was a Greek philosopher who lived in the 4th century BCE and is considered one of the most important figures in Western philosophy. He was a student of Plato and tutored Alexander the Great, and his ideas have had a profound influence on a wide range of fields, including ethics, politics, biology, and metaphysics.

27. The Greek island of Rhodes is home to the famous Colossus of Rhodes, one of the Seven Wonders of the Ancient World.

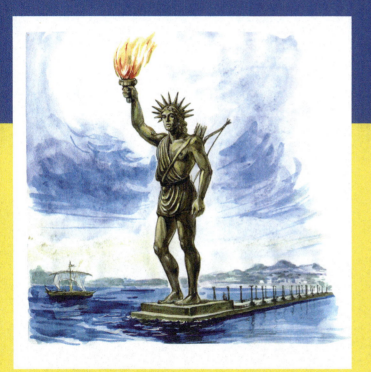

The Colossus of Rhodes was a gigantic bronze statue of the Greek god Helios that stood at the entrance to the harbor of Rhodes, one of the Seven Wonders of the Ancient World.

28. Greece has over 300 days of sunshine per year.

29. Greece is home to the most archaeological museums in the world.

Pictured Acropolic Museum

30. Christianity is largest religion in Greece.

Religion in Greece is dominated by the Greek Orthodox Church.

Pictured The Byzantine Church

31. Greece has a Mediterranean climate with mild, wet winters and hot, dry summers.

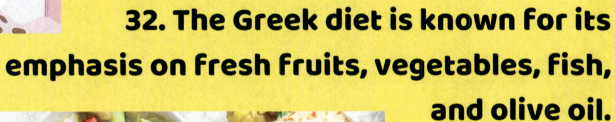

32. The Greek diet is known for its emphasis on fresh fruits, vegetables, fish, and olive oil.

33. Football is the most popular sport in Greece.

34. There are more than 4,000 traditional dances in Greece.

DID YOU KNOW?

Kalamatianos is the national dance of Greece.

35. The Battle of Marathon, where the Greeks defeated the Persians in 490 BCE, inspired the modern-day marathon race.

The Treasury of Athens was was built to commomerate Greek victory in the Battle of Marathon.

Pictured Treasury of Athens

36. The Trojan War, as recounted in Homer's epic poem The Iliad, took place in ancient Greece.

37. The Greeks developed the concept of tragedy in theater, with playwrights like Aeschylus, Sophocles, and Euripides.

38. Greece has a long and rich history of wine production, dating back over 4,000 years.

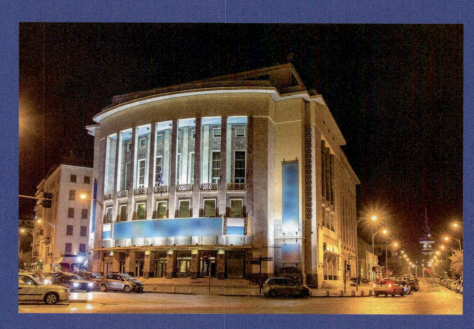

39. Greece is one of the world's most popular countries to visit.

Did You Know?

Greece welcomed around 31 million international visitors in 2019, making it one of the top tourist destinations in the world.

40. Athens has more theatres than any other city in the world.

41. Greece has over 120 million olive trees and produces 2.2 million metric tons of olives every year.

42. The Haliacmon is longest river flowing entirely in Greece.

43. Native animals of Greece include brown bears, wolves, lynx, goats and donkeys.

44. Greece is home to a diverse range of wildlife, including a variety of mammals, birds, reptiles, and marine animals.

45. The national animal of Greece is the dolphin.

46. The national bird in Greece is the little owl.

47. Greece is the world's largest producer of natural sponges.

48. Greek staple foods include bread, grains, potatoes, pasta, eggplant, cucumbers, tomatoes, lentils, yogurt and feta cheese.

49. Popular Greek dishes include Fasolatha, Koulouri, Loukoumades, Souvlaki, Dolmades, Spanakopita and Gyros.

50. The Greek alphabet has 24 letters, with the first letter being alpha (A) and the last being omega (Ω).

51. Greece has a parliamentary system of government, with a president as the head of state and a prime minister as the head of government.

52. The Greek word "democracy" comes from two Greek words: demos, meaning "people," and kratos, meaning "power" or "rule."

Words from Greece

- The Greek word "olympic" comes from the ancient Greek word "Olympia,"
- The Greek word "philosophy" means "love of wisdom,"
- The word "alphabet" comes from the first two letters of the Greek alphabet, alpha and beta.

53. Greece has a rich tradition of folk music, with regional variations in style and instruments used.

54. The Greek island of Crete is home to the Palace of Knossos, one of the most important archaeological sites from the Minoan civilization.

55. The Greek flag's blue and white colours are said to represent the sea and waves.

How many flags can you recognise?

56. Greece has a high level of seismic activity due to its location on the boundary of two tectonic plates.

57. The Greek island of Zakynthos is home to the famous Navagio Beach, which is known for its crystal-clear waters and shipwreck.

58. The Greeks invented the concept of citizenship, with the idea that citizens had certain rights and responsibilities.

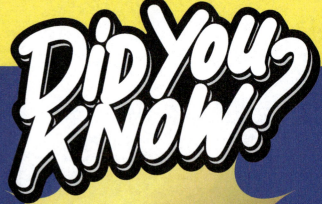

Navagio beach gets its name from the shipwreck of a smuggler's boat called the Panagiotis, which ran aground on the beach in 1980 while carrying contraband cigarettes.

59. Greece has a rich tradition of pottery, with many unique styles and techniques developed over thousands of years.

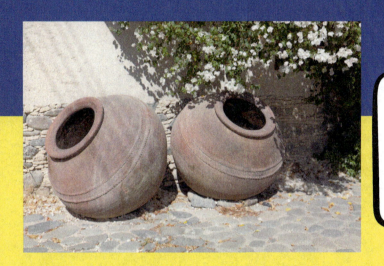

Greek pottery was often decorated with intricate designs featuring scenes from mythology, everyday life, and nature. The style of Greek pottery varied over time and was influenced by different regions and cultures, such as the Minoans and Mycenaeans.

60. Greece has a large shipping industry, with one of the largest merchant fleets in the world.

Places To Go

Places To Go

Are you ready to go on an adventure to Greece? Get your passports ready, grab your camera, and let's explore the most amazing places in Greece! From the ancient ruins of the Acropolis to the stunning beaches of Santorini, we'll discover the treasures of this beautiful country. Get ready to learn about the myths and legends that surround these magical places, and imagine yourself walking in the footsteps of the gods and goddesses of ancient Greece. So come on, let's pack our bags and get ready to embark on an unforgettable journey to Greece!

Santorini: This picturesque island is famous for its stunning sunsets, unique architecture, and volcanic beaches. Visitors can also explore ancient ruins and taste the island's delicious cuisine.

Crete: The largest of the Greek islands, Crete has something for everyone, from stunning beaches and rugged mountains to ancient ruins and traditional villages.

Nafplio: This charming coastal town in the Peloponnese region is known for its well-preserved Venetian architecture, quaint streets, and scenic views of the sea.

Delphi: Delphi is a UNESCO World Heritage Site located on the slopes of Mount Parnassus. It was once home to the famous oracle of Apollo and is considered one of the most important archaeological sites in Greece.

Rhodes: The island of Rhodes is home to many historic landmarks, including the medieval Old Town, the Palace of the Grand Master of the Knights of Rhodes, and the ancient Acropolis of Lindos.

Mykonos: This popular island in the Aegean Sea is known for its picturesque white-washed buildings, beautiful beaches, and vibrant nightlife.

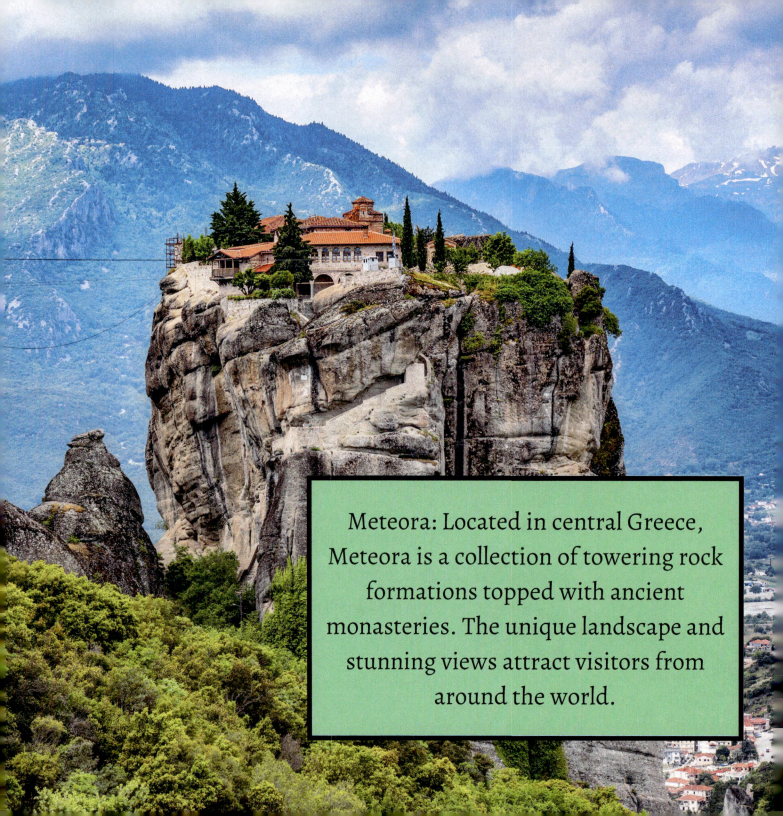

Meteora: Located in central Greece, Meteora is a collection of towering rock formations topped with ancient monasteries. The unique landscape and stunning views attract visitors from around the world.

Acropolis of Athens: One of the most famous landmarks in Greece, the Acropolis is an ancient citadel located on a rocky outcrop above the city of Athens.

Corfu: Corfu is a stunning island in the Ionian Sea known for its beautiful beaches, crystal-clear waters, and lush vegetation. It's also home to a number of historical landmarks, including the Old Fortress and the Palace of St. Michael and St. George.

Hydra: This picturesque island is known for its charming harbour, narrow streets, and traditional stone houses. Visitors can explore the island's museums and galleries, take a scenic boat tour, or hike to the top of Mount Eros for panoramic views.

Peloponnese: This large peninsula is home to many of Greece's most famous historical sites, including the ancient city of Olympia, the fortress town of Mycenae, and the UNESCO-listed Byzantine city of Mystras.

Thessaloniki: The second-largest city in Greece, with a rich history and cultural heritage, including the stunning Byzantine churches and the White Tower.

Zagori: A region of traditional stone villages, winding rivers, and lush green forests, known for its hiking trails and natural beauty.

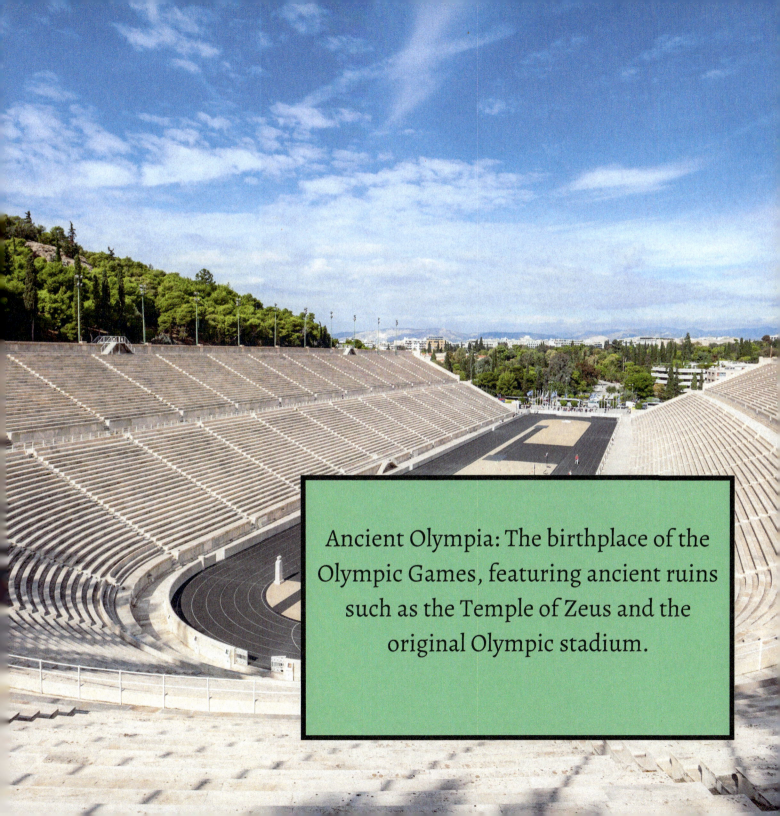

Ancient Olympia: The birthplace of the Olympic Games, featuring ancient ruins such as the Temple of Zeus and the original Olympic stadium.

Explore

Explore

The "Explore?" section is a fun way to test your knowledge about Greece. You can answer trivia questions about the country, its history, culture, and traditions. See how many you can get right and challenge your friends and family to see who knows the most. Don't worry if you don't know the answer to every question, because you can always learn something new by reading this book again and exploring more about Greece. Have fun!

Test Yourself

What is the capital city of Greece?
Answer: The capital city of Greece is Athens.

What is the most famous building in Athens?
Answer: The most famous building in Athens is the Acropolis.

What is the name of the sea that surrounds Greece?
Answer: The sea that surrounds Greece is called the Aegean Sea.

What is the name of the famous temple in Athens that was built to honour the goddess Athena?
Answer: The famous temple in Athens that was built to honour the goddess Athena is called the Parthenon.

Test Yourself

What is the name of the famous ancient Greek philosopher?
Answer: Socrates.

What is the name of the famous ancient Greek mathematician?
Answer: Pythagoras.

What is the name of the famous ancient Greek playwright?
Answer: Sophocles.

What is the name of the famous statue in the island of Rhodes?
Answer: The Colossus of Rhodes.

What is the name of the famous ancient site that used to be a city?
Answer: The Acropolis.

Activities To Try

Activities

Welcome to the Activities section! Here, you'll find a variety of fun and engaging activities related to Greece. Each activity is designed to help you explore different aspects of Greek culture and history in a hands-on way. Whether you want to create your own Greek mask, try some traditional Greek foods, or learn some Greek dances, we've got you covered. We encourage you to try out as many of these activities as you like, and don't be afraid to put your own spin on them. Use your creativity and imagination to make them your own! So, get ready to have some fun and learn about Greece in a new way.

Create Your Own Olympic Games

Materials needed:
Open outdoor space or indoor area with enough room for racing
Markers or chalk to mark start and finish lines
Optional: small prizes or medals for the winners

Instructions:
1. Choose a few different types of races that you want to include in your mini Olympics, such as a sprint, relay race, potato sack race, or three-legged race.
2. Set up your race course by using markers or chalk to mark start and finish lines. Make sure to measure the distance of the race course to ensure it's fair for all participants.
3. Assign a referee or timer to keep track of each race and determine the winners. You can also have other participants cheer on the racers and create a festive atmosphere.
4. Line up the participants at the starting line and give them clear instructions for the race, such as "On your mark, get set, go!"
5. Once the race is over, declare the winner and award them with a small prize or medal. You can also take a photo of the winners and create a mini medal ceremony to celebrate their achievement.
6. Repeat the process for each type of race that you want to include in your mini Olympics.
7. At the end of the mini Olympics, tally up the number of wins for each participant and declare an overall winner.

Remember to have fun and be a good sport, whether you win or lose. The most important part of the mini Olympics is having fun and enjoying the spirit of friendly competition!

Greek Dancing

Materials needed:
Access to Greek music
A device to watch instructional videos on

Instructions:
1. Find a space where you can move around freely, like a living room or a backyard.
2. Choose some Greek music to dance to. You can find traditional Greek music on YouTube or other music streaming platforms.
3. Watch some videos online to learn the steps for traditional Greek dances like the Kalamatianos or the Syrtos.
4. Practice the steps with your family or friends until you feel comfortable with them.
5. Put on some music and have a Greek dance party!

The most important part of this activity is having fun and enjoying the spirit of dance!

Create a Greek island collage

Materials needed:
Magazines and newspapers
Printed images of Greek islands
Scissors
Glue
Construction paper or cardboard

Instructions:
1. Collect magazines, newspapers, and printed images that feature pictures of Greek islands. You can also print images from the internet.
2. Cut out the images that you like and arrange them on a piece of paper or cardboard to create your collage.
3. Use glue or tape to attach the images to the paper or cardboard.
4. Add any other decorations you like, such as stickers, markers, or glitter.
5. Display your Greek island collage proudly!

The most important part of this activity is having fun and being creative!

Greek food tasting

Materials needed:
Tzatziki
Feta cheese
Olives
Grape leaves
Other traditional Greek foods you would like to try
Small plates
Utensils

Instructions:
1. Choose a selection of traditional Greek foods to try, like tzatziki, feta cheese, olives, and grape leaves.
2. Set up a mini mezze platter with each food item arranged on a plate or tray.
3. Invite your family or friends to join in the tasting and try each food item together.
4. Talk about the flavours and textures of each food item, and which ones you like best.
5. Enjoy your Greek food tasting party!

The most important part of this activity is having fun and trying new flavours!

Make a Greek temple

Materials needed:
Cardboard
Markers
Paint
Paintbrushes
Scissors

Instructions:
1. Gather materials like cardboard, markers, paint, scissors, and glue.
2. Cut out a large rectangle from the cardboard to serve as the base of the temple.
3. Cut out smaller rectangles to create columns and pediments for the temple.
4. Decorate the columns and pediments with markers and paint to make them look like marble.
5. Glue the columns and pediments onto the base to create your Greek temple.
6. Add any other decorations you like, such as gold stickers or glitter.
7. Display your Greek temple proudly!

The most important part of this activity is having fun and getting creative!

Greek mythology storytelling

Materials needed:
Your favorite Greek myths and legends (books or online resources)
Your imagination
A storytelling voice and an eager audience

Instructions:
1. Choose a Greek myth or legend to read with your family or friends. You can find collections of Greek myths for kids at your local library or bookstore.
2. Take turns reading the story out loud or use different voices for different characters.
3. After you finish reading, talk about the story and ask each other questions about the characters and events.
4. Create your own Greek story by taking turns adding new characters and events to the story.
5. Have fun and let your imaginations run wild!

The most important part of this activity is having fun and using your imagination!

Glossary

Glossary

Acropolis - A citadel or fortified area built on a high hill in ancient Greece, usually containing important buildings and temples.

Aegean Sea - A large body of water located between Greece and Turkey.

Democracy - A system of government in which the people have a say in decision-making through elections and representation.

Goddess - A female deity, often associated with nature, fertility, and wisdom.

Mythology - A collection of myths and stories belonging to a particular culture, often involving gods, goddesses, and supernatural creatures.

Olympics - An international sporting event that originated in ancient Greece and is now held every four years.

Philosopher - A person who seeks wisdom and knowledge through rational thought and reflection.

Polis - A city-state in ancient Greece that was the basic political unit.

Sparta - A city-state in ancient Greece known for its militaristic society and strict way of life.

Zeus - The king of the gods in Greek mythology, often associated with thunder and lightning.

Author's Note

Dear young readers,

I am so excited to have shared with you all about Greece, a country that is rich in history, art, mythology, and culture. As an author, I am always inspired by the incredible diversity and beauty of the world around us, and I hope this book has inspired you to explore and learn more about Greece.

I was inspired to write this book because I believe that learning about different cultures and countries can help us understand and appreciate the world better. It's so important to celebrate and learn from different traditions and ways of life, and I hope this book has helped you do just that.

If you enjoyed reading this book, I would love it if you could leave a review on Amazon. Reviews help other readers discover the book and can make a big difference for independent authors like myself.
Thank you for joining me on this journey, and I hope this book has sparked your curiosity and imagination. Keep exploring and learning about the world around you!

Sincerely,
Grant Publishing

Printed in Great Britain
by Amazon